The Magic Ocean 2

Ron Lokkesmoe

This book is the second part of a collection of photographs of the ocean and inspirational messages that give them meaning.

I dedicate this book to my wife, Barbara.
She truly loves the ocean!

FIRST EDITION Printed in the United States of America
Copyright 2014 - Ron Lokkesmoe

ISBN-13: 978-1502537812
ISBN-10: 1502537818

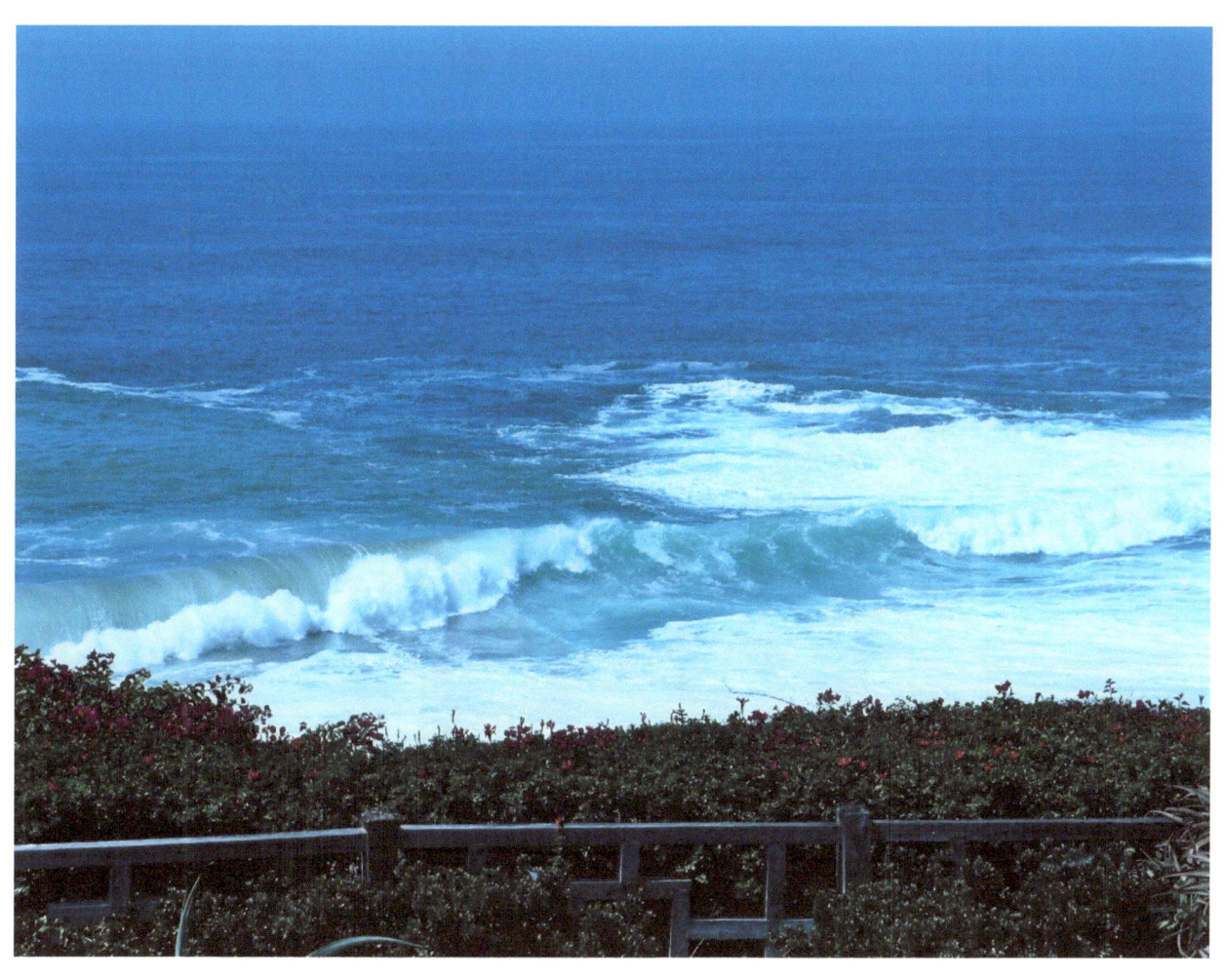

The Magic Ocean 2

Ron Lokkesmoe

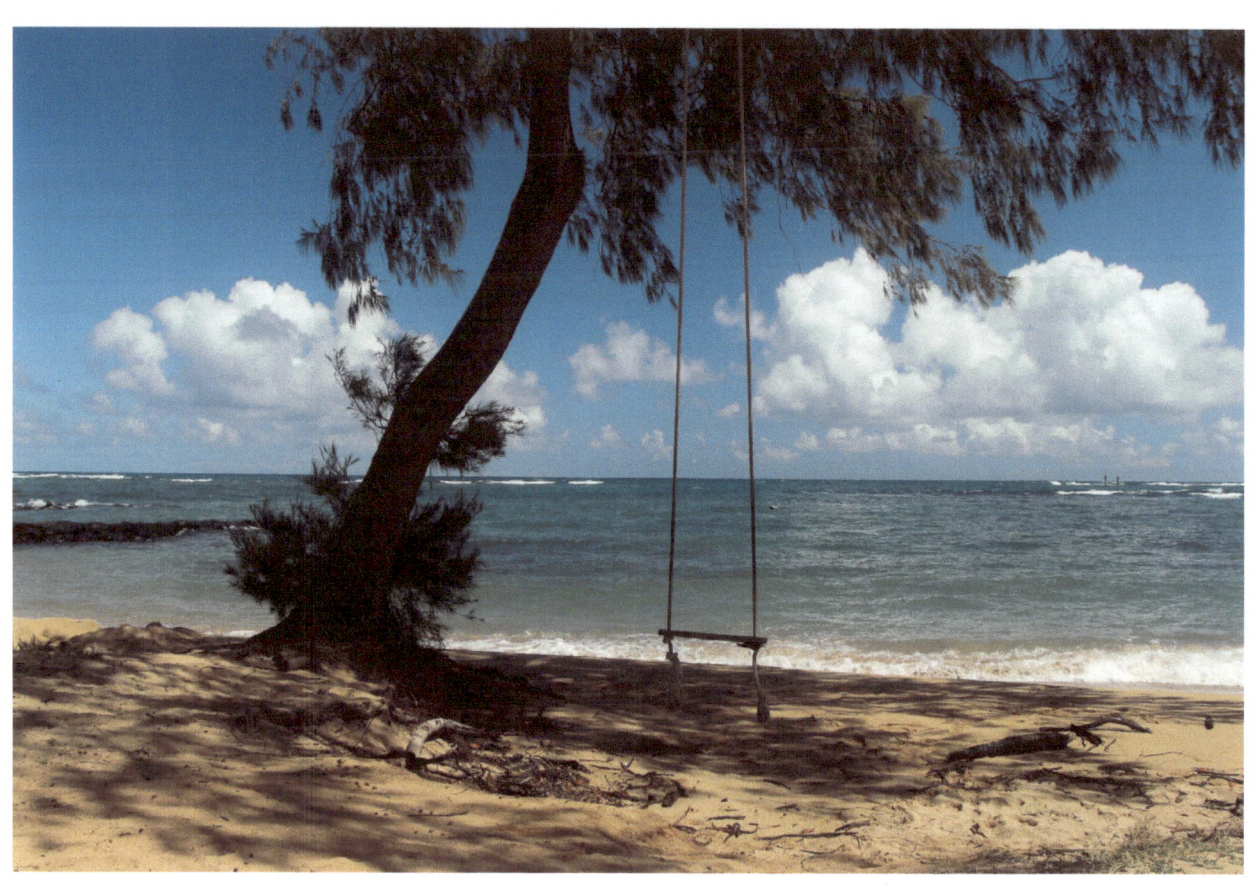

May the ocean bring you peace of mind.

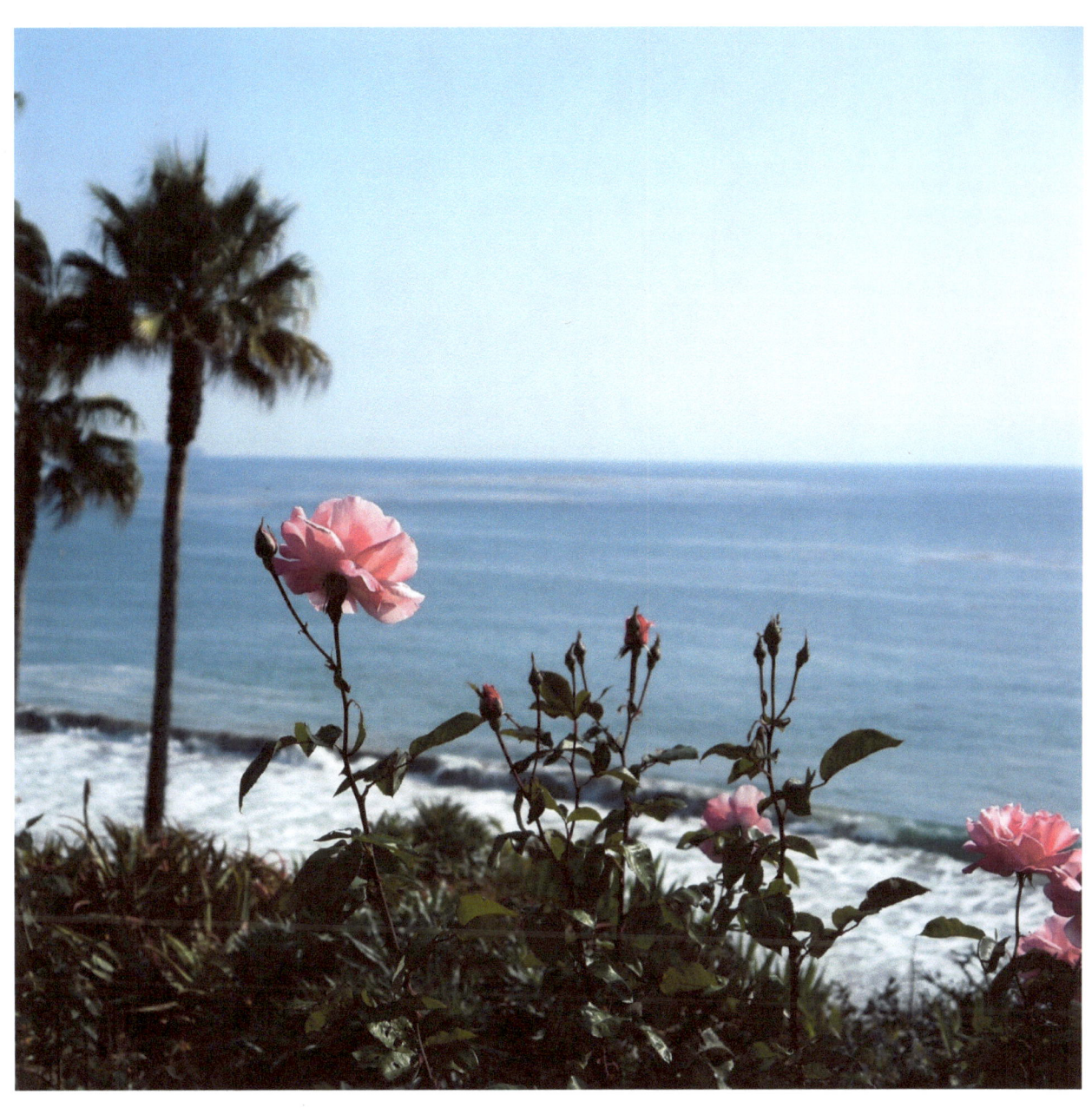

The ocean has a magic all its own.

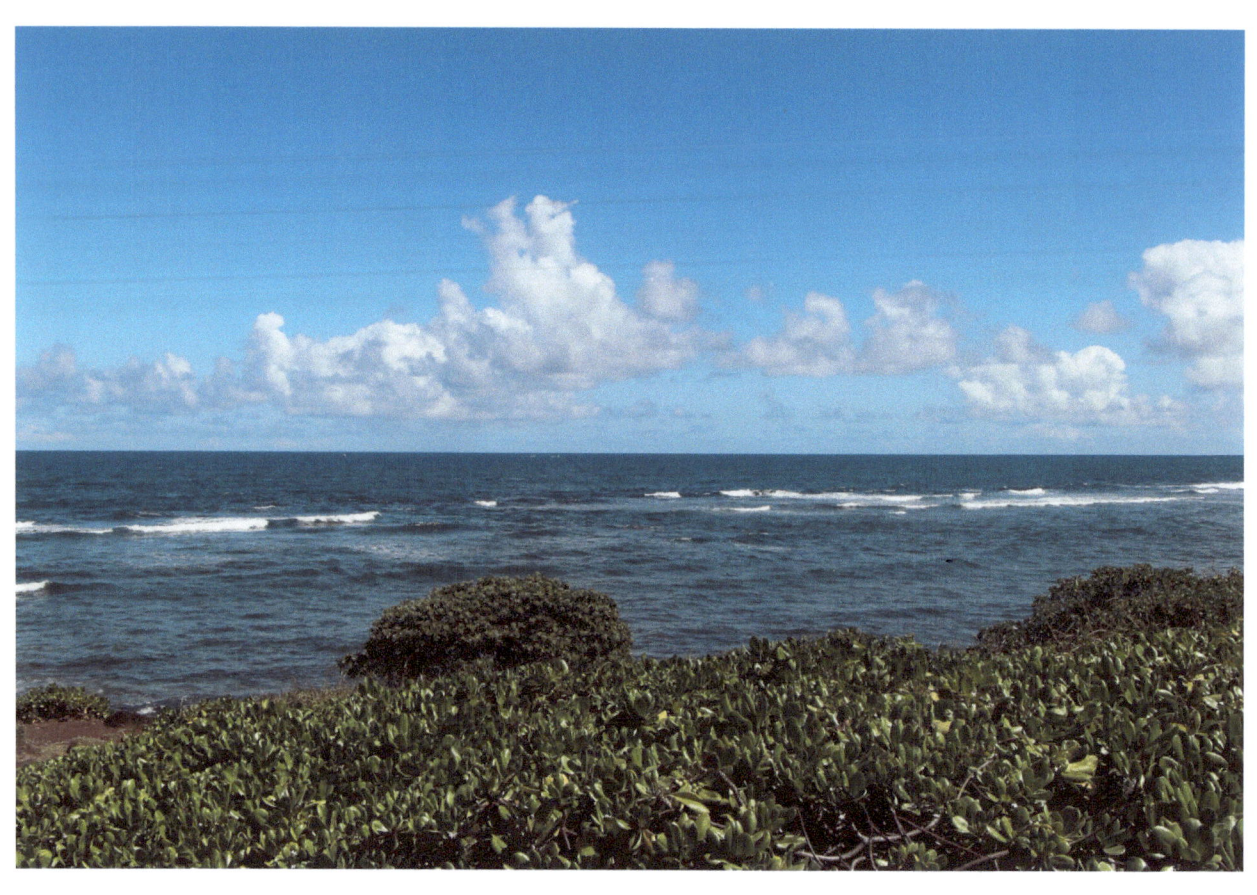

The ocean can be magnificent!

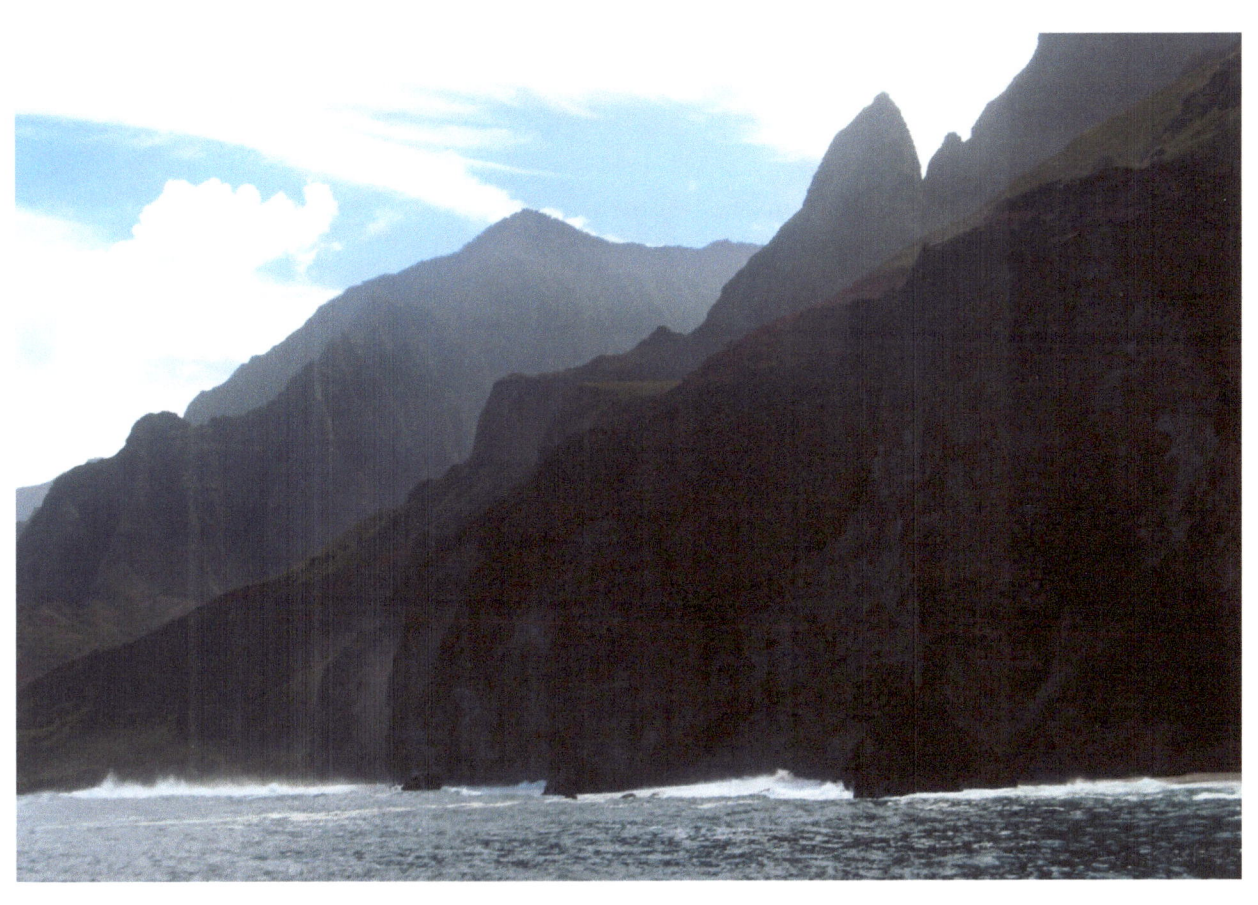

The ocean can be mystifying.

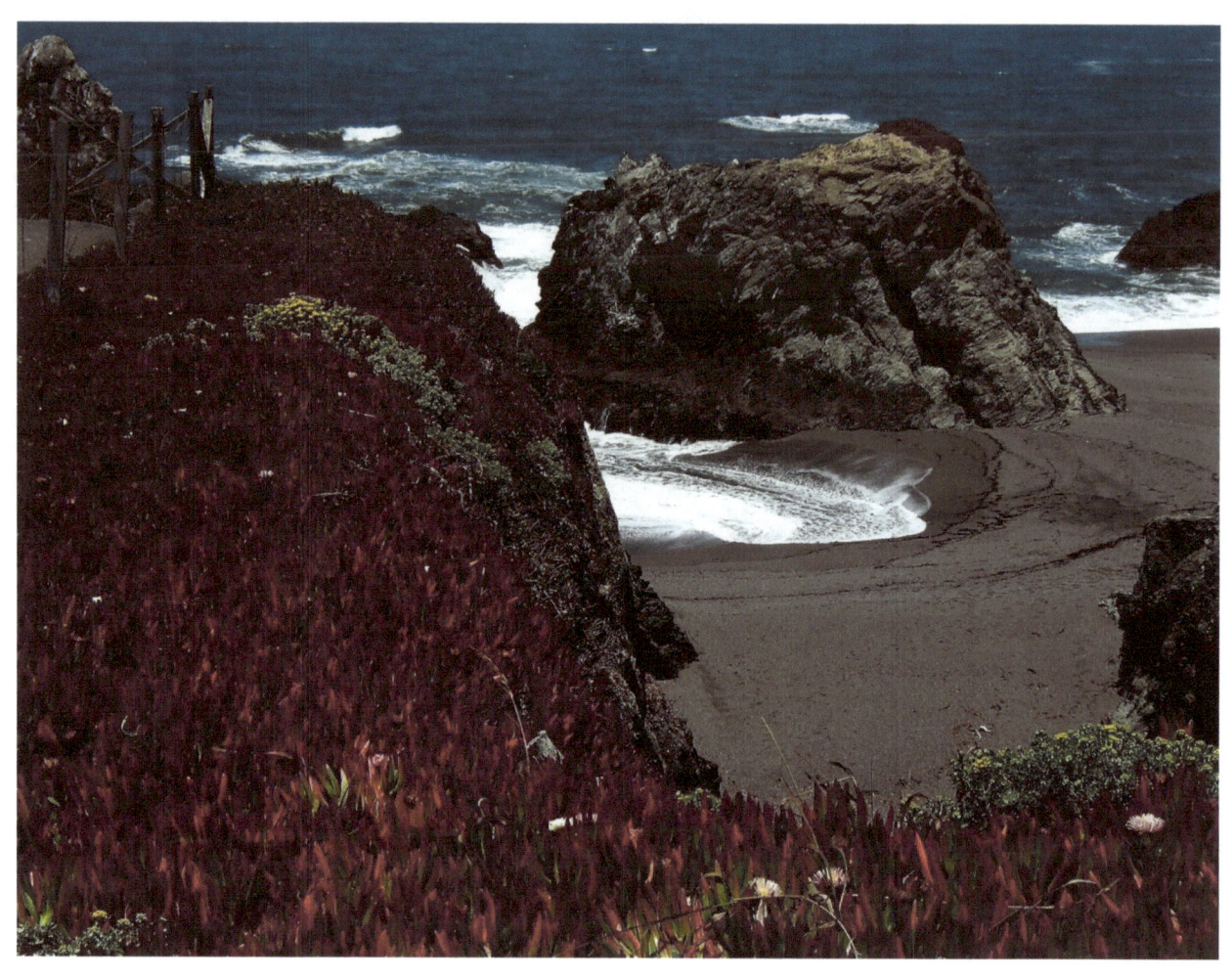

The ocean can renew your soul.

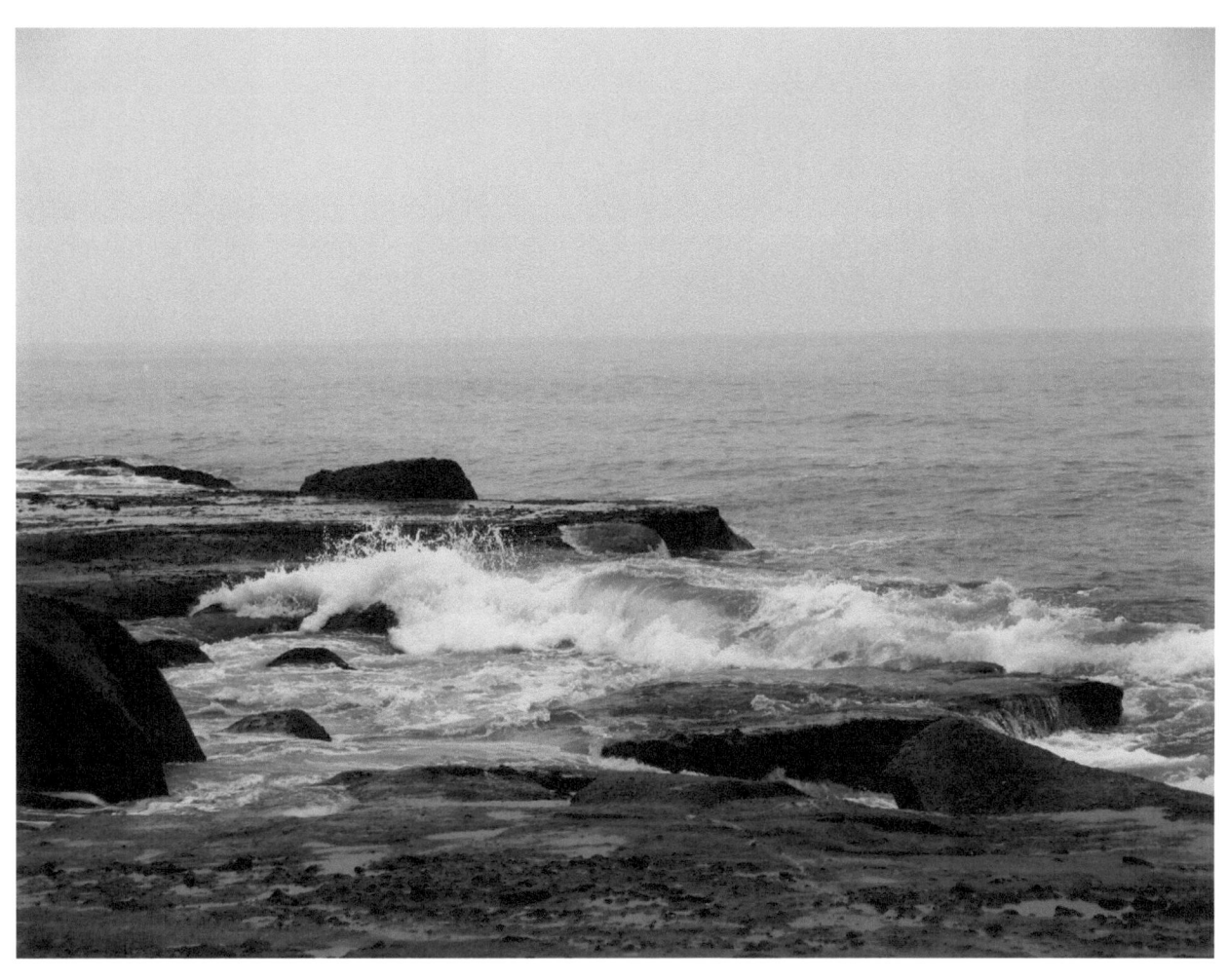

The ocean has moods, just like humans.

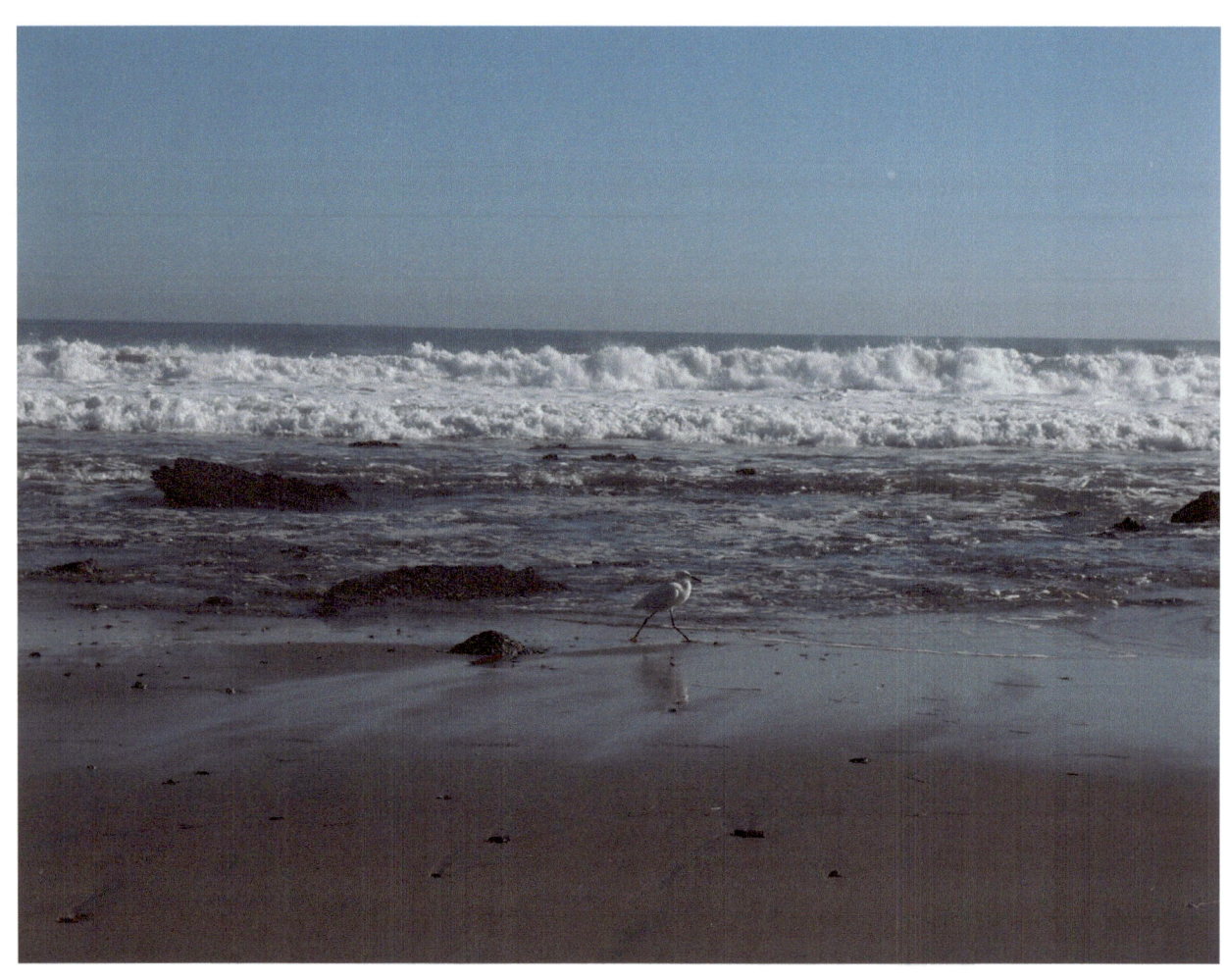

There is nothing better than a walk along the beach.

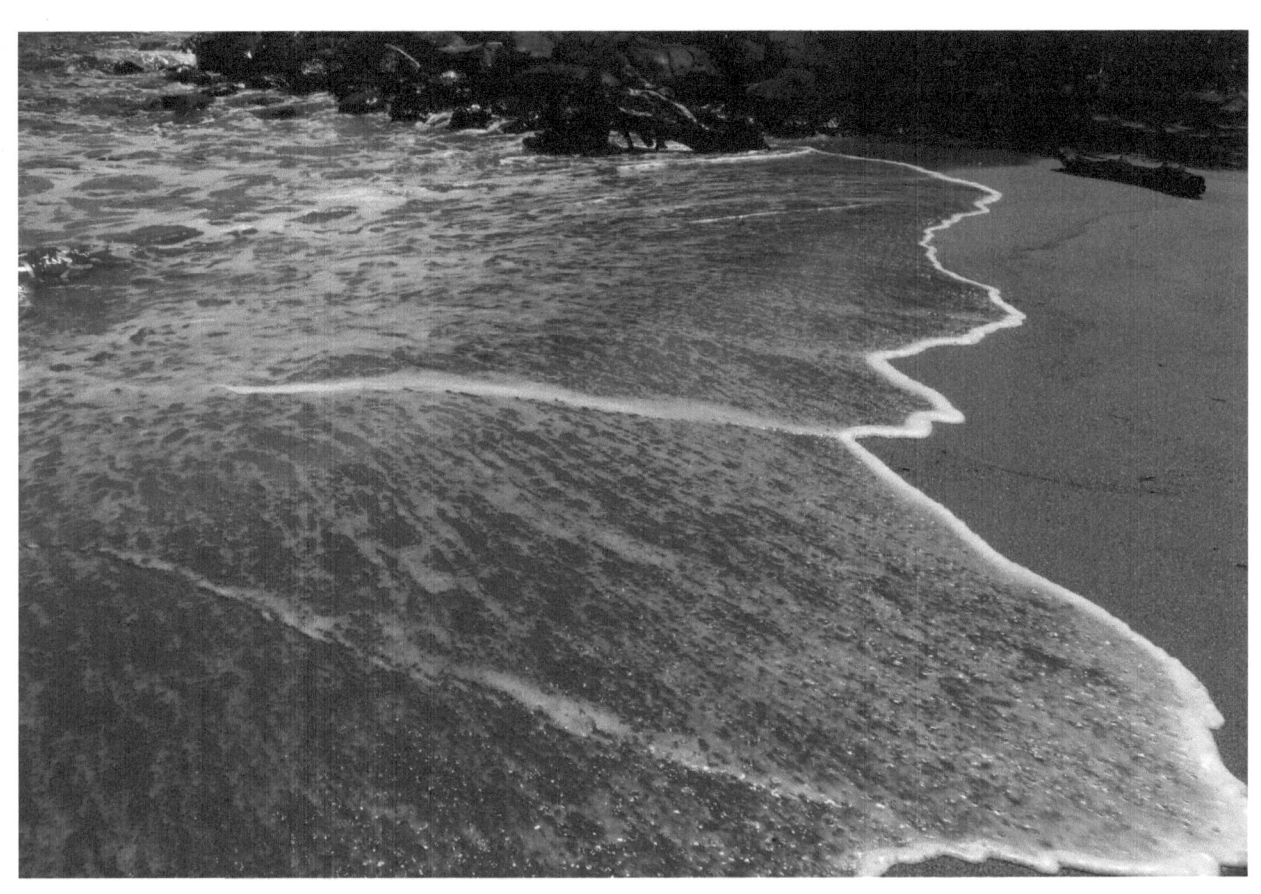

When you are overwhelmed, go to the ocean.

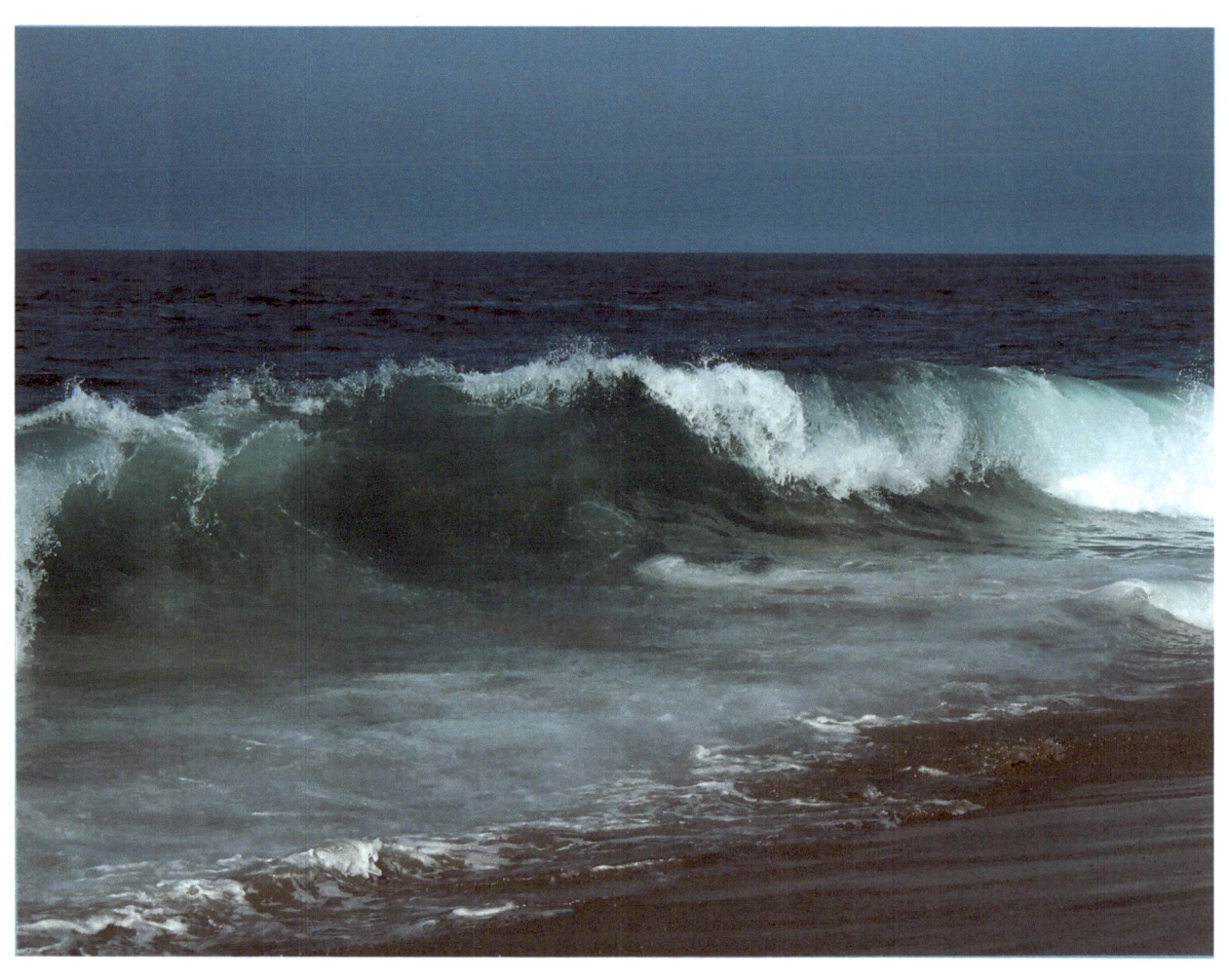

It is part of our nature to be drawn to the ocean.

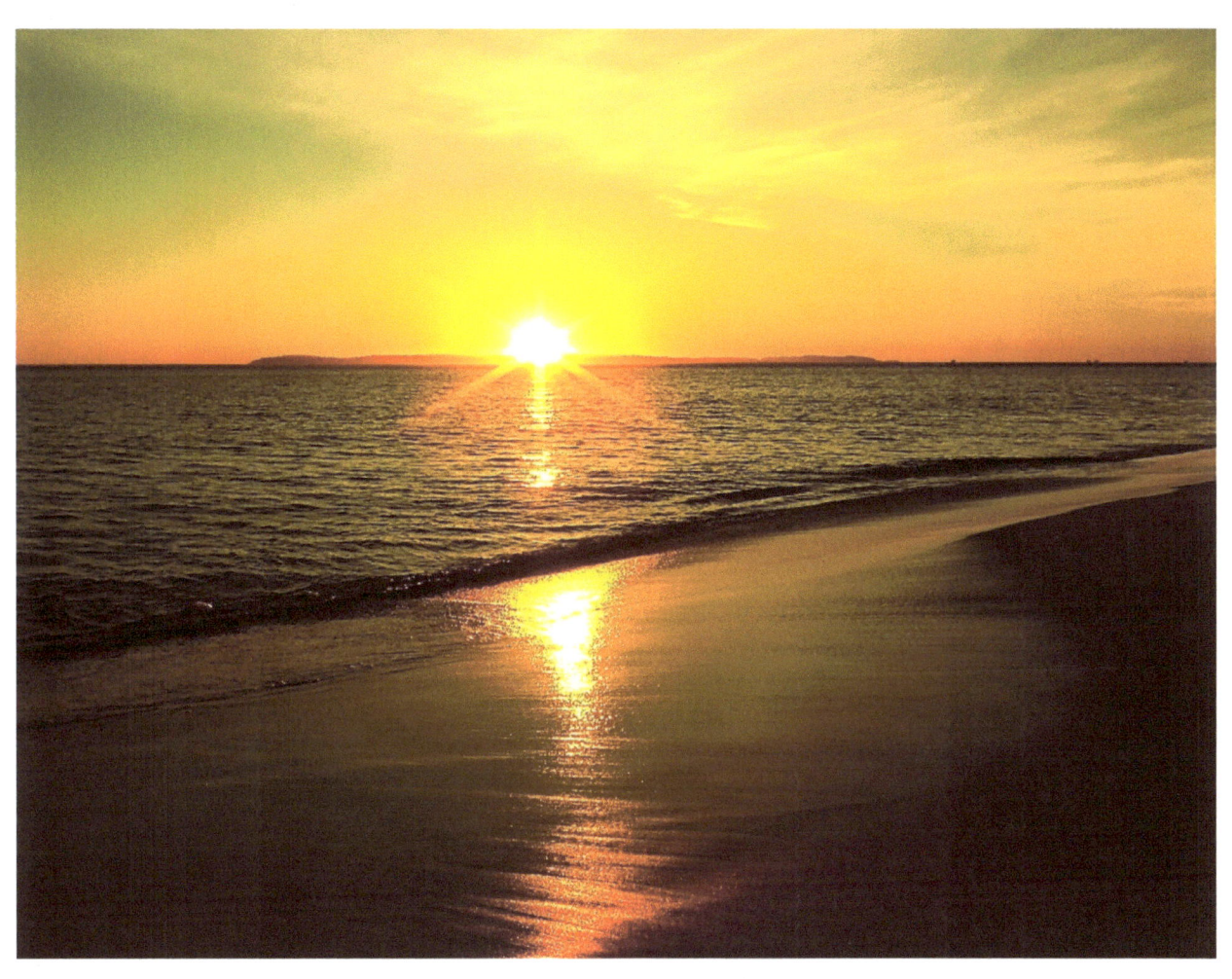

The ocean can be warm and wonderful!

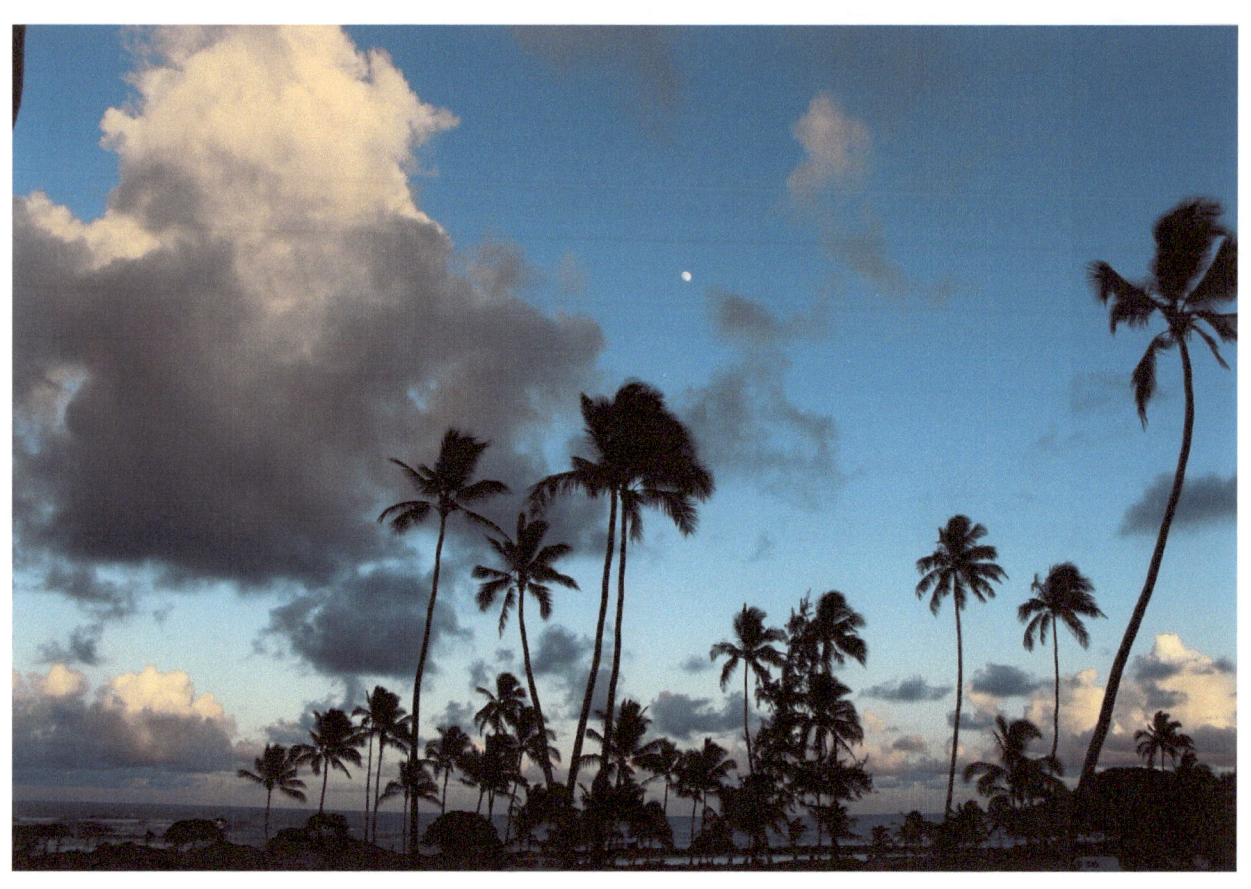

You can gaze at the moon and stars at the ocean.

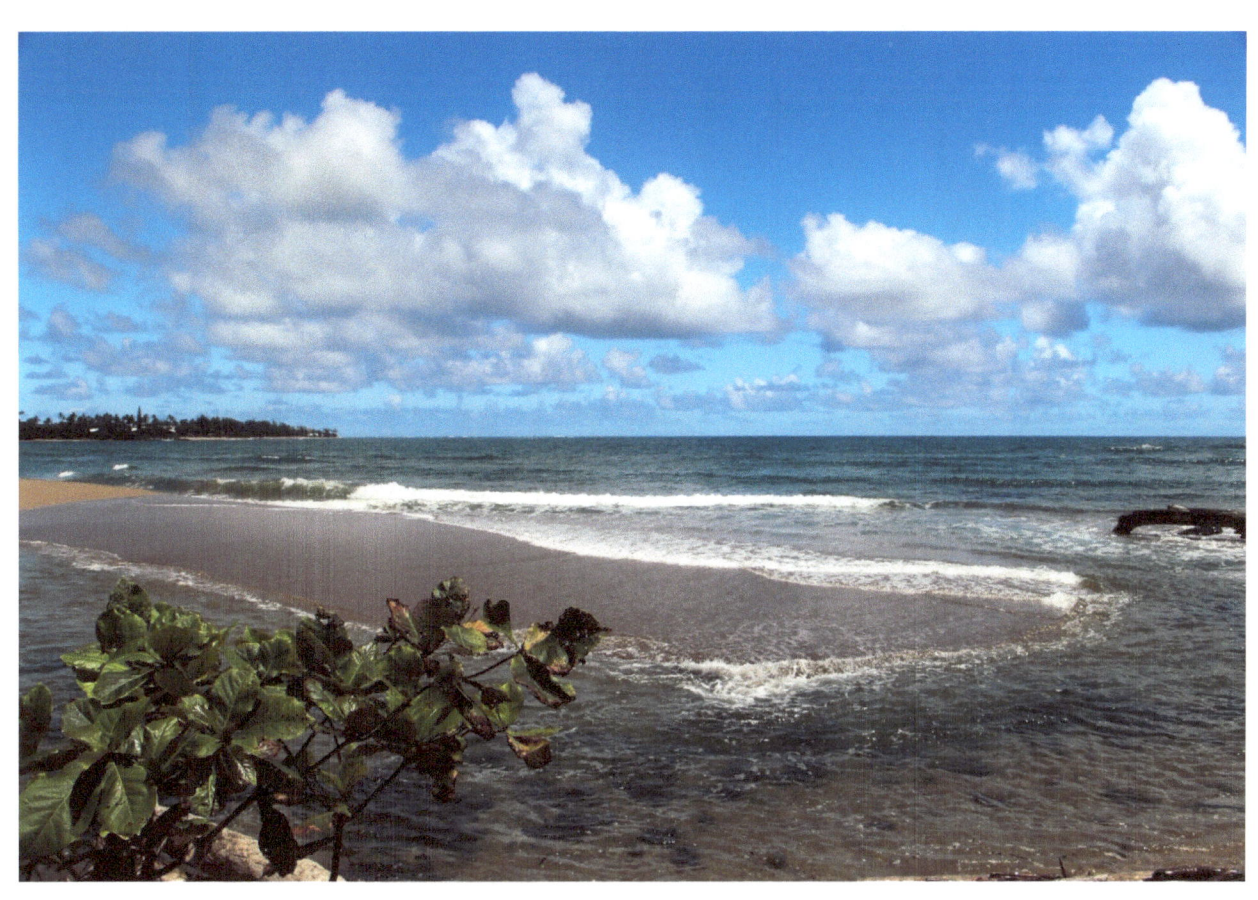

Every day is the best day at the ocean.

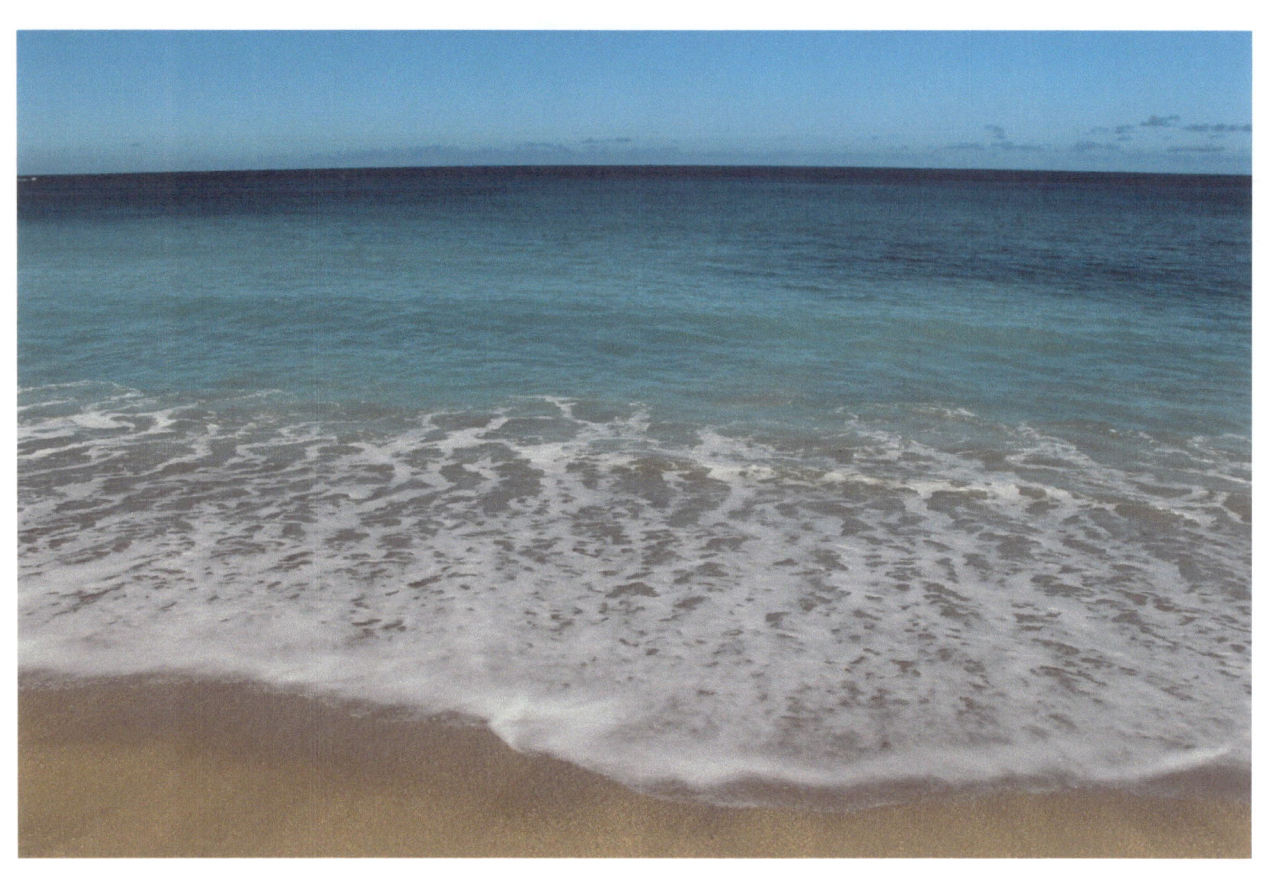

Find the beauty of nature at the ocean

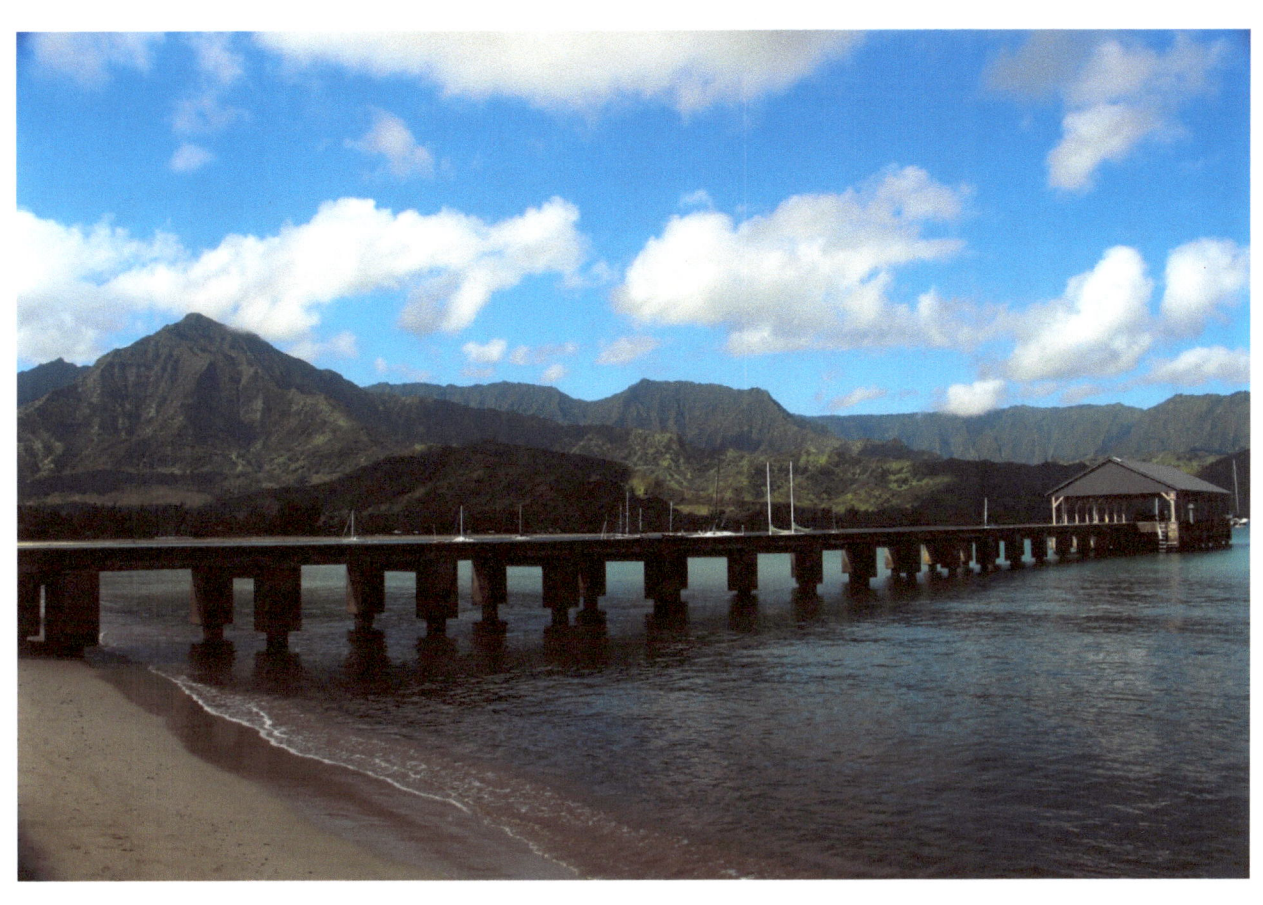

Walk upon the warm waters.

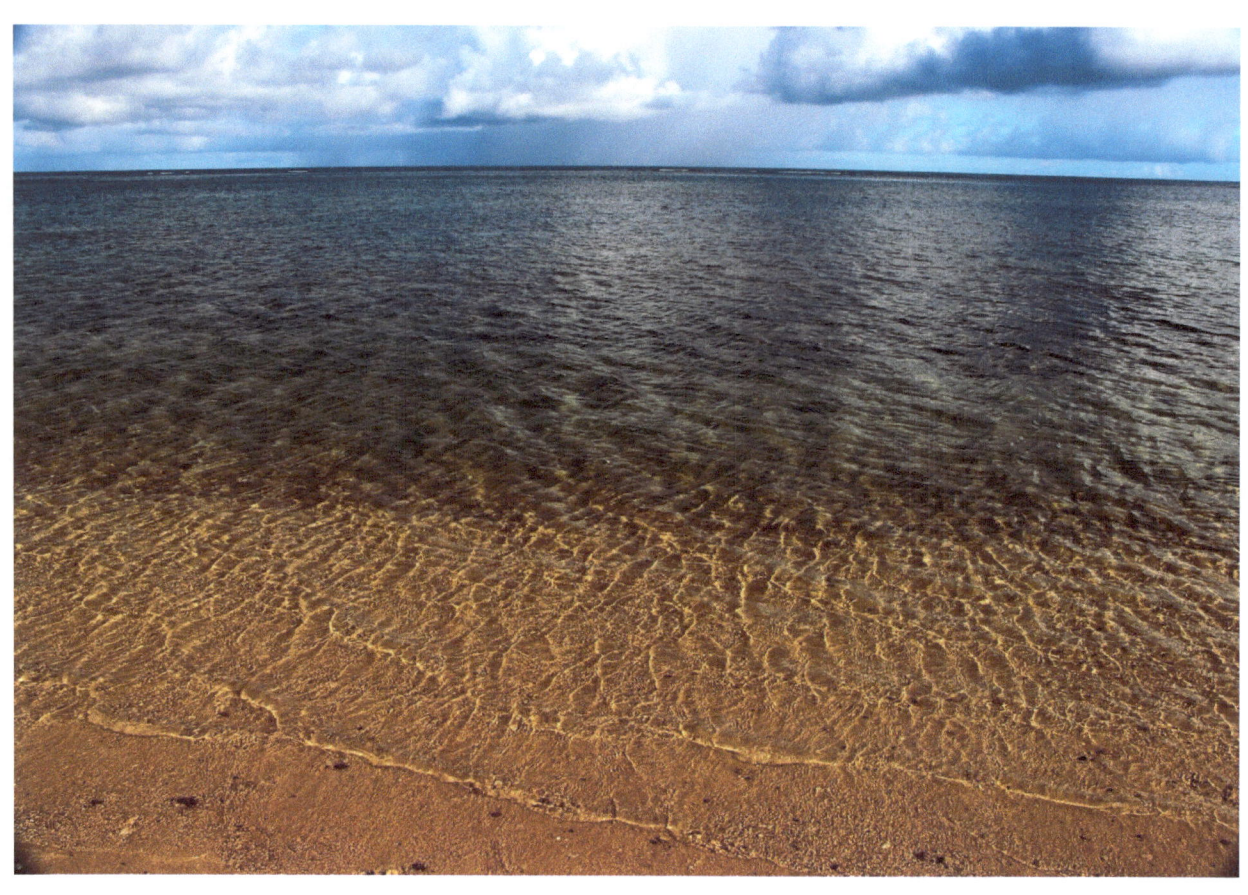

Let your feet enjoy the gentle waves.

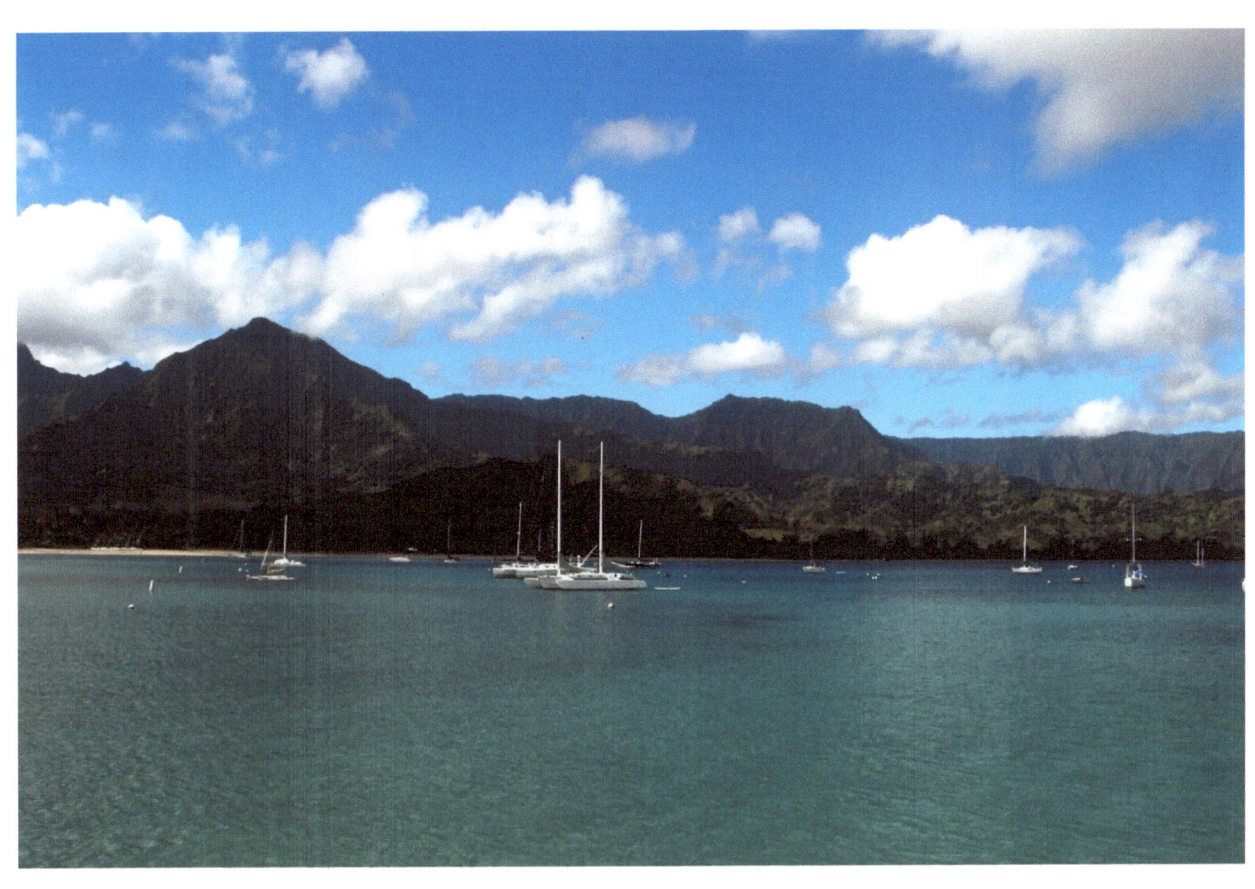

Let your mind set sail.

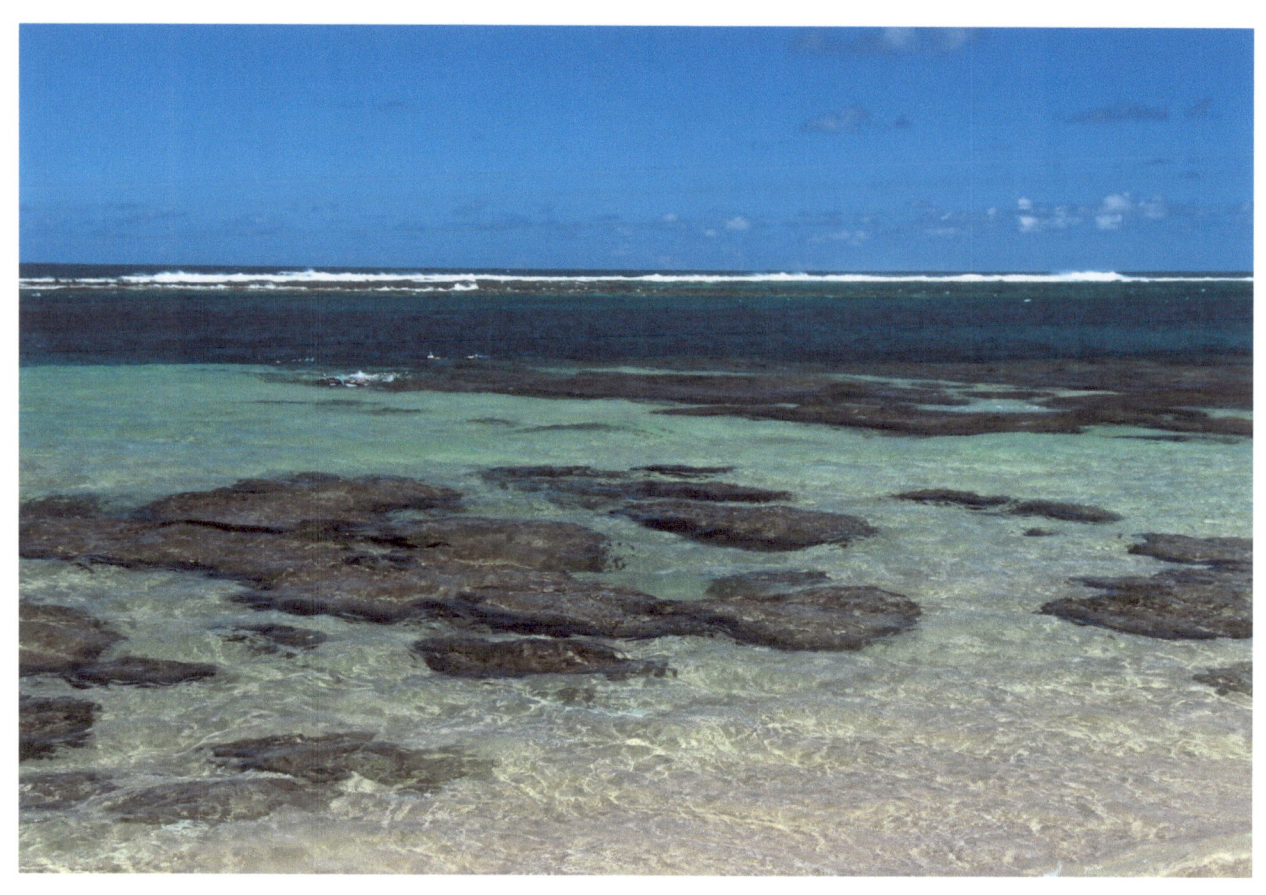

Drift in a quiet bay.

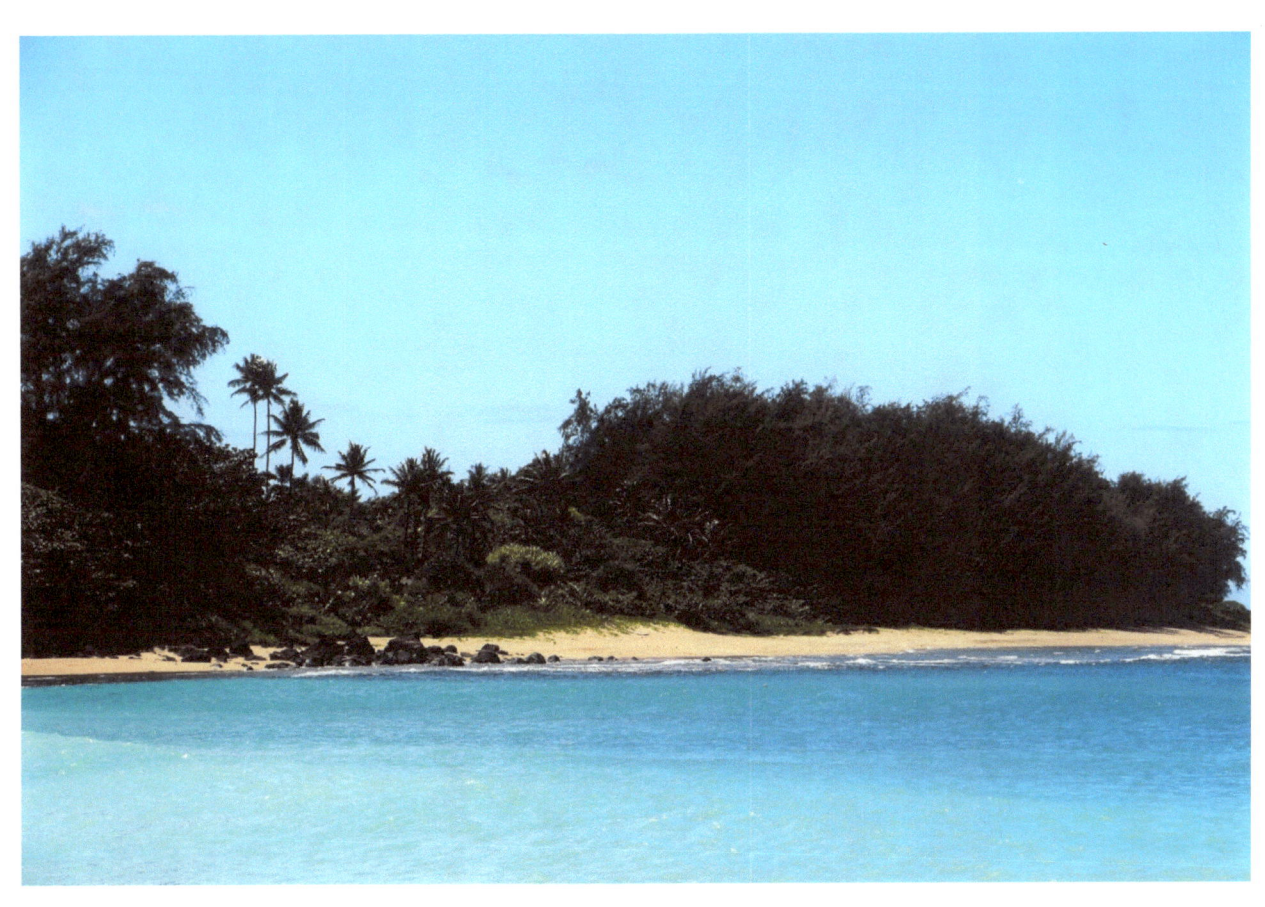

The perfect beach waits for you.

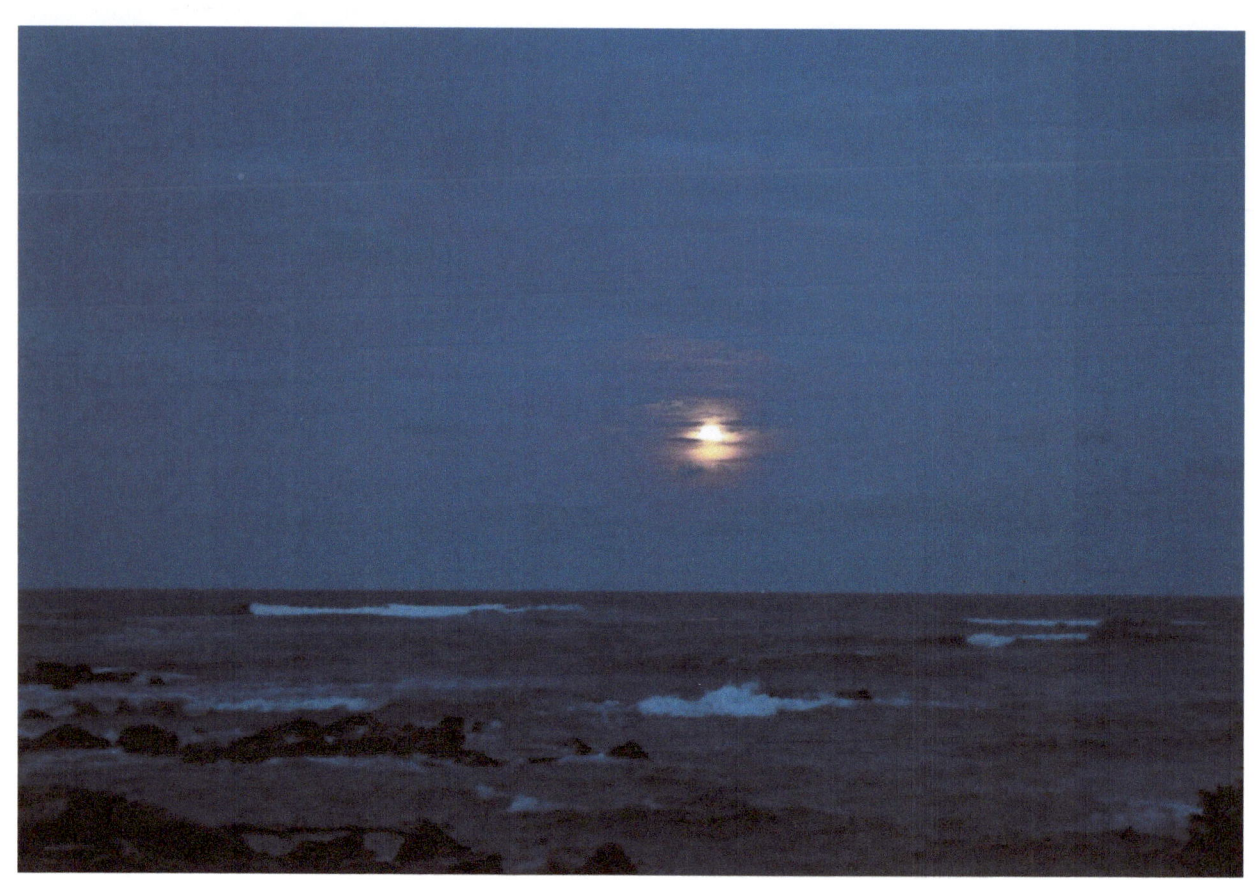

The ocean has its mystery.

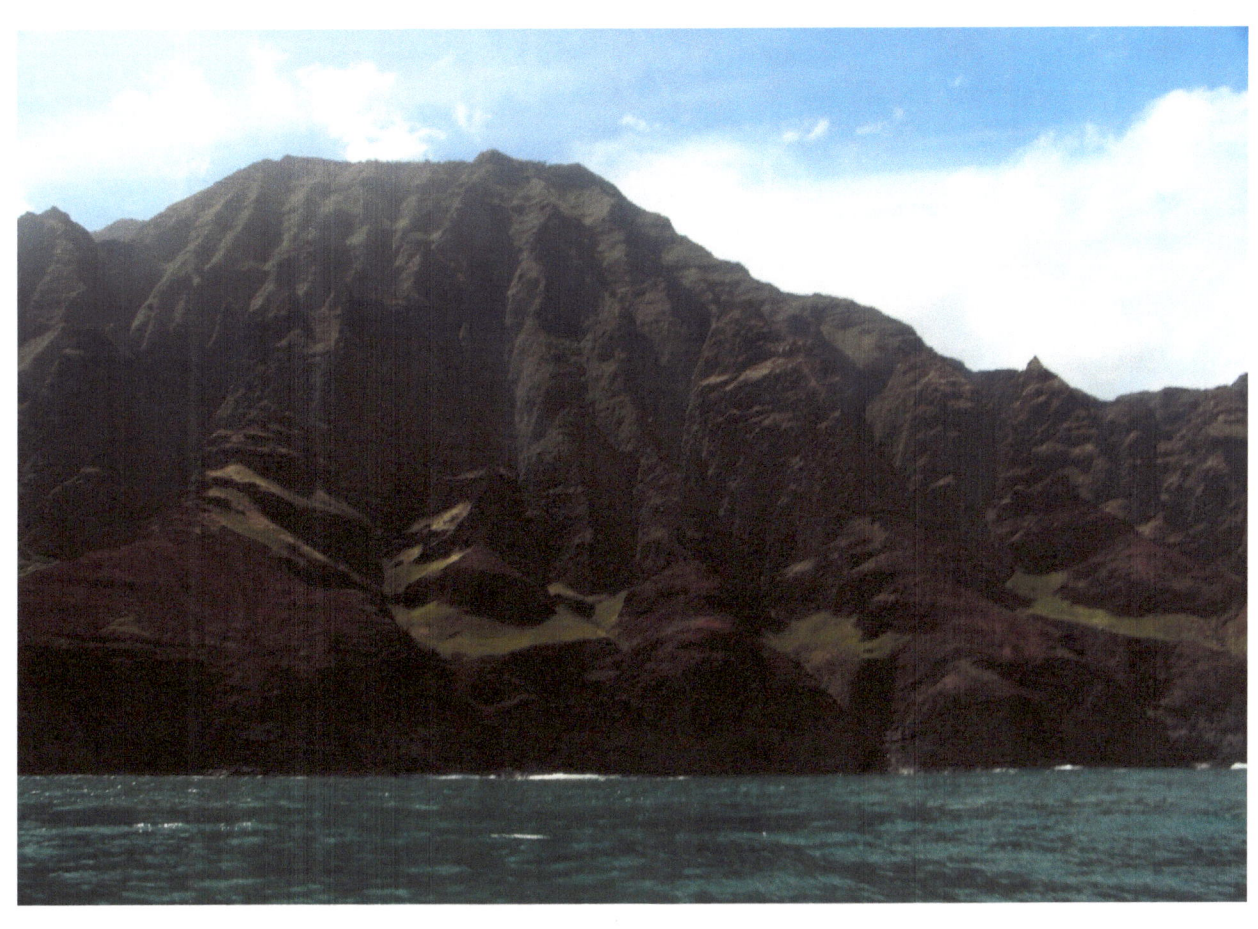

The beautiful Kauai coast!

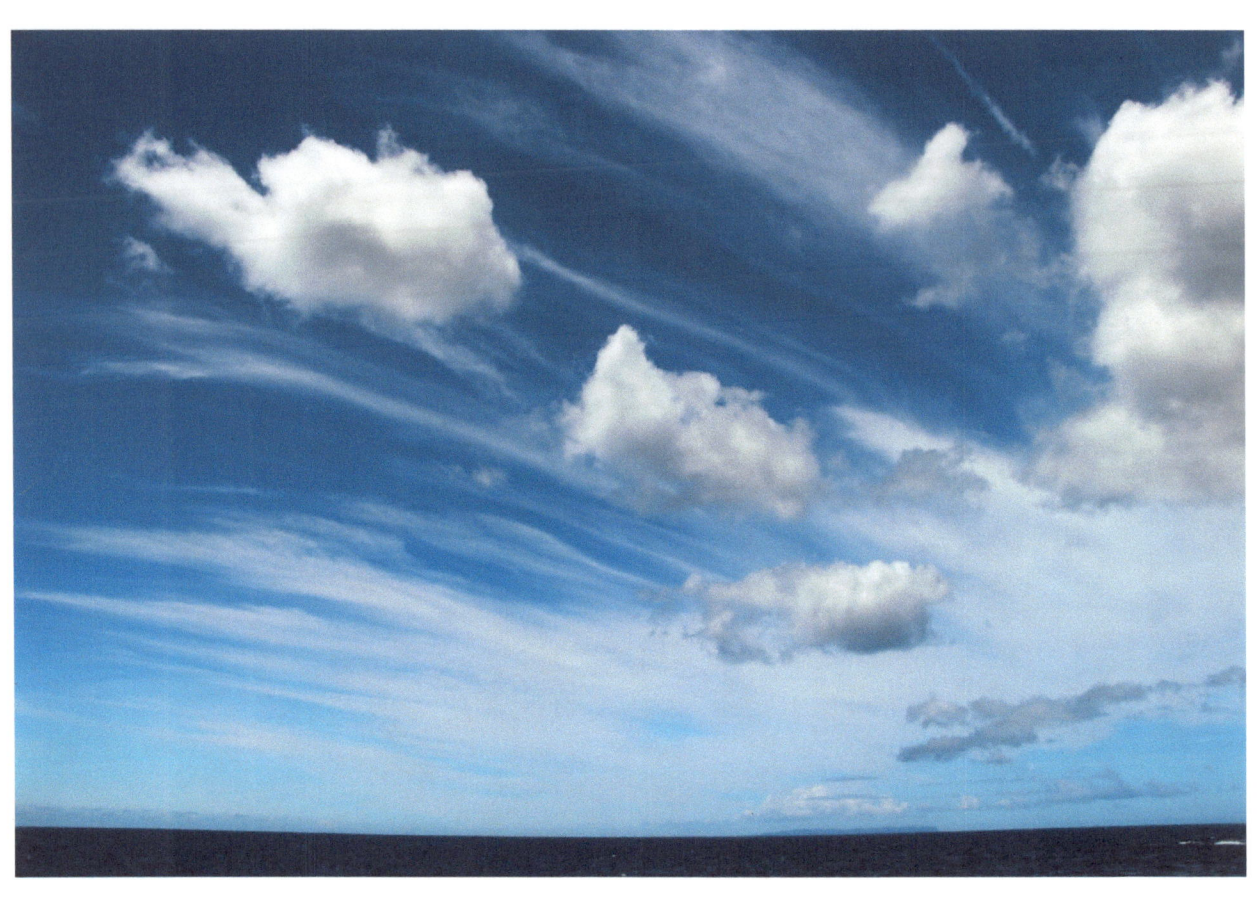

The sky meets the sea.

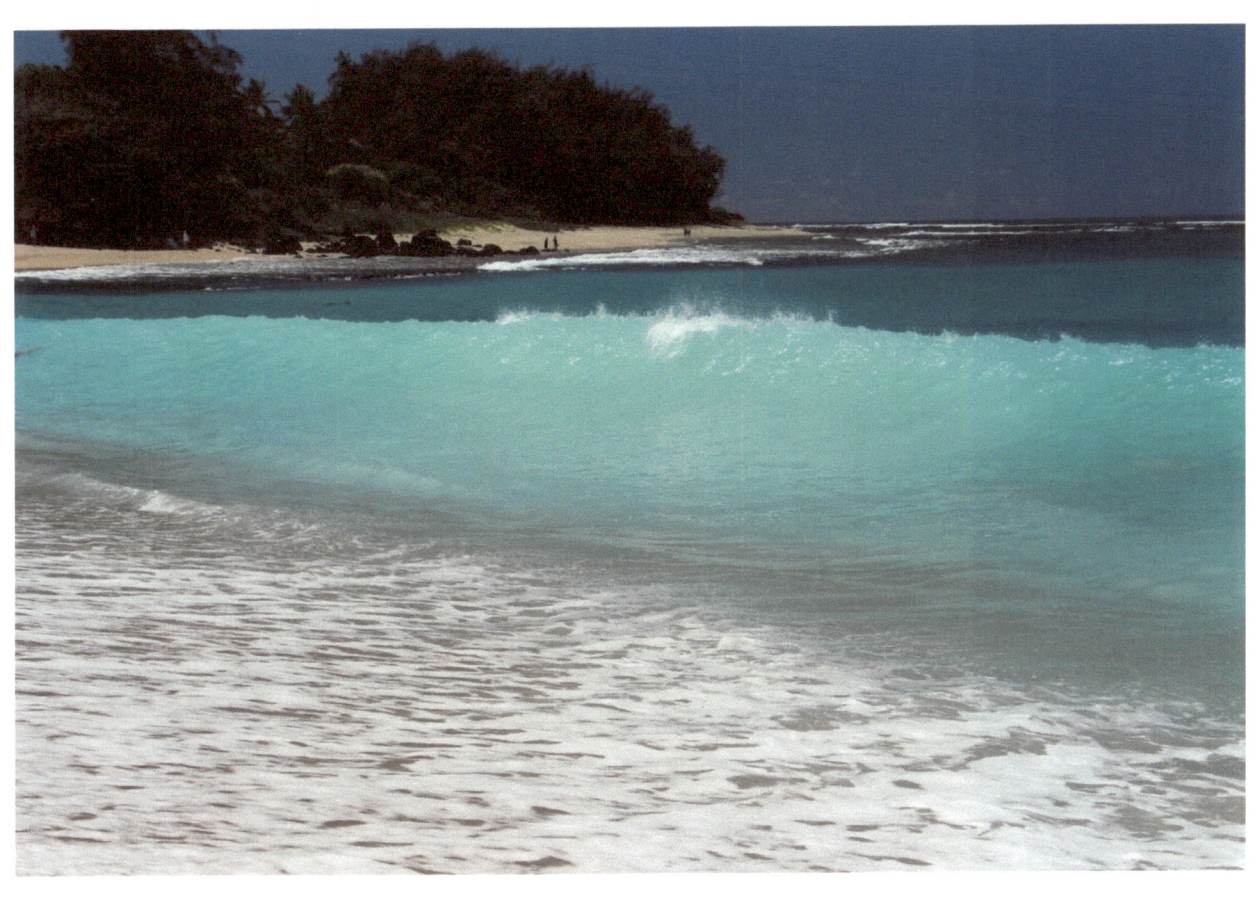

A wave is a wonderful thing.

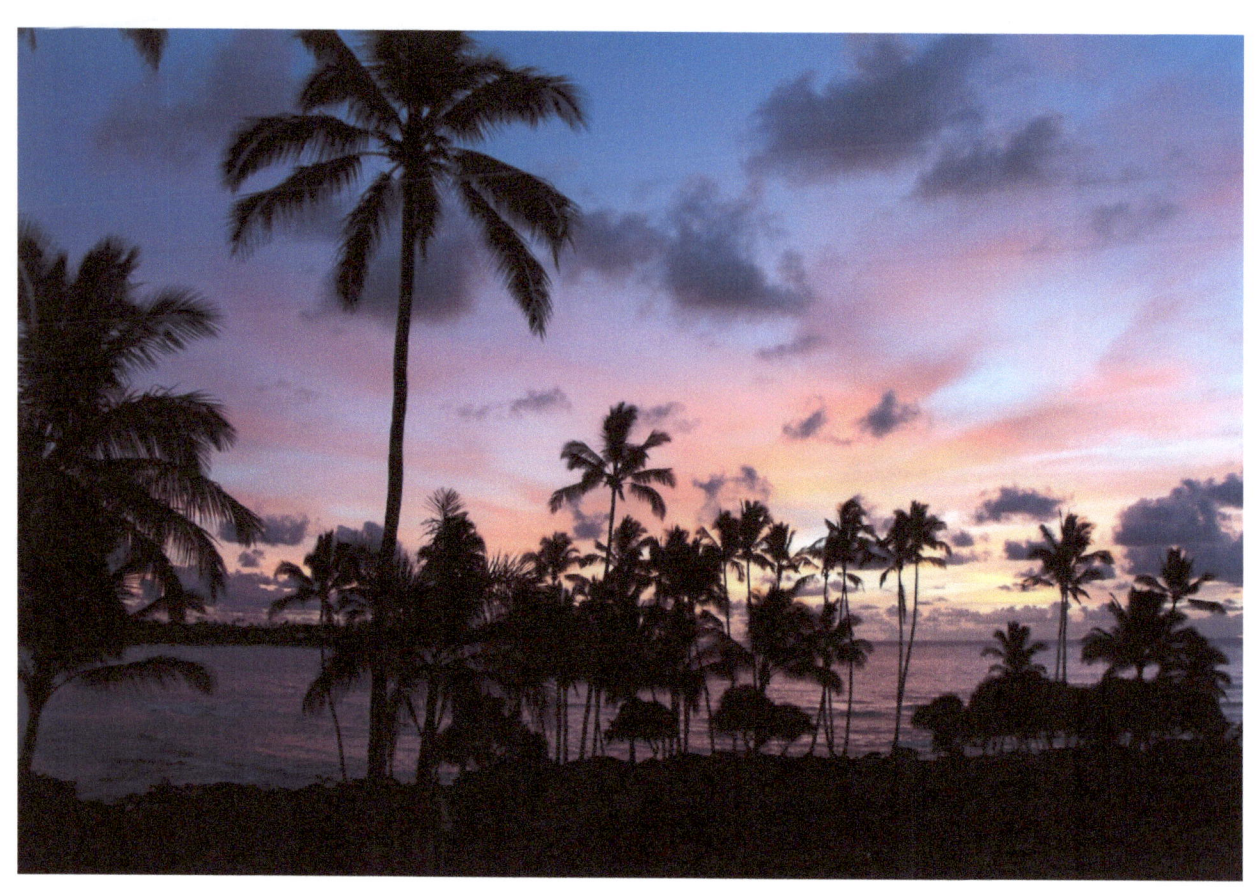

Another day in paradise.

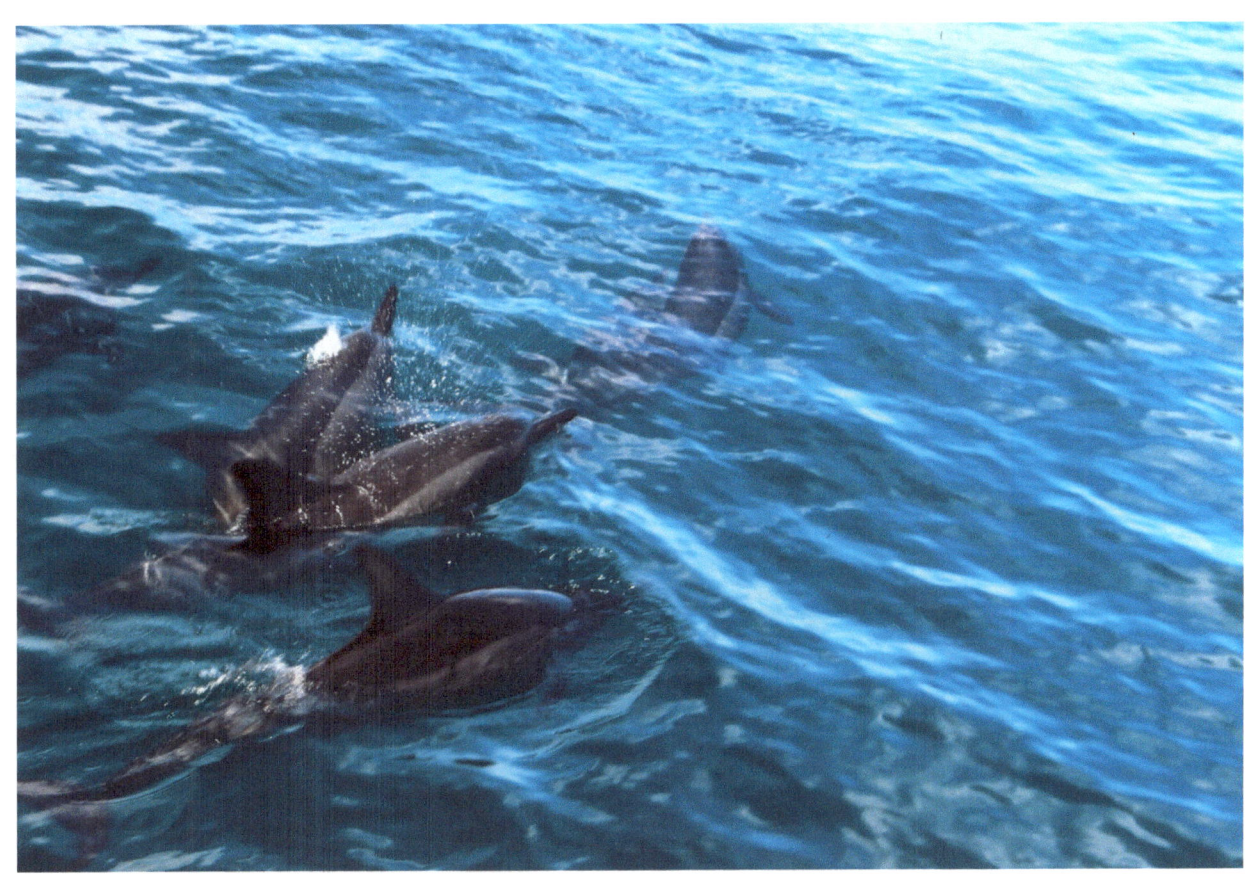

The ocean is a place to play.

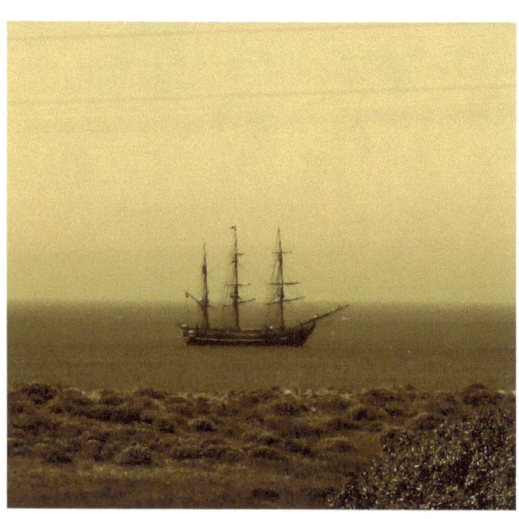

Photographs and inspirational messages

created by Ron Lokkesmoe

RonLokk@gmail.com

www.ingramcontent.com/pod-product-compliance
Lightning Source LLC
Chambersburg PA
CBHW050425180526
45159CB00005B/2416